Thornwork

Thornwork

Ruth Baumann

Black
Lawrence
Press

Black
Lawrence
Press

www.blacklawrence.com

Executive Editor: Diane Goettel
Book Design: Amy Freels
Cover Design: Zoe Norvell
Cover Art: "Tree lady, burn out" by Chantal Fortin

Published 2020 by Black Lawrence Press.
Printed in the United States.

grateful acknowledgment to the journals which first published these pieces, sometimes in varying forms:
Colorado Review: Between Seasons; Getting Over
Heavy Feather Review: In Absentia
Jellyfish: Coming of Age; Volta
The Fem: Portrait: Maternal Instinct ['Has the phone been ringing']

for Julia & Teddy,
queens of ferocity, loyalty, & love

thank you for showing me
new parts of my heart

Contents

III. Summers, Springs

I.

Falls, Winters

Volta

Lightning like a fist to the face. Is this the morning of the imagination?

I dress in the dark & live in the dark. I employ a narrative

of fog & no absolution. Weather, like feelings, is scenery. Then the slow

climb. The shock wave of a pause. Everything on broken glass

is my heaven, until the weird day when I recognize

I might hold a candle for my species. *Language may not matter to you*

if you've always been able to use it, I think. In my head, my thoughts

take on affectations, this one a mixture of venom & a sweet

southern drawl. Like *bless your heart*. That's what I mean, but

a little less. The broken glass will be there. This chance at softness will not.

Pardon my need, pardon its need for a choir, a church, a can of gasoline.

To Return to One Start

There were several spaces to lie down, but I chose, as always, a floor.
Sandwiched my body between one cold & another.

The first man I thought I loved had eyes like the sky popping out of its
    frame.
Too bad his veins were the same.

Later he found me but it wasn't important, then, except to disrupt
another man I was pretending with, a snail-ride to hell.

I can't tell you what's at stake until you listen.

When J turned his slow laugh towards me, I thought,
oh. & for a long time, *oh* was good enough,

a little heavy & a little hungry on the tongue all at once.
& for a long time, *oh* was good enough,

a little heavy & a little hungry on the tongue all at once.
J understood my need for a really moveable sleep.

———

J tattooed his own hands in middle school, disappeared for months,
said *sorry, I was getting over meth, can we date again*?

I clocked his long fingernail. I nodded anyway.
What's a loss besides an opportunity for repetition?

I can't tell you what's at stake until you know there's other.
Later his pupils little birds so far gone the wings didn't even show.
Later no wings, no wings. *Oh*.

———

& for a long time, *oh* was good enough,
a little heavy & a little hungry on the tongue all at once.

I failed so many languages.
J! What ideas, what flicker of body heat against mine in a park.

We were young & god, we weren't right.
But how else could we be? Do tornadoes raise clear skies?

Do tornadoes raise up more than they destroy?

This is the easier, softer way, I was told,
upon the entrance to an exit years later.
J's ghost like sandpaper like fleas like sandpaper fleas on my tongue.
No, he's still alive. Somewhere

I'm letting every J touch me, again, their barely lit bodies
pressing hands all over. Somewhere I always will be,

even post-, even with a stake in survival.

This is how the world works:
in every way it ever has, still.

Oh. Those rabbit pulses, those slow-murk pulses. *Oh*.

Oh. More.

Small Failures

Once when
I was seventeen
&
had the shakes,
I
looked up at
the sun.

I didn't make
that
mistake again
for years.

Sometimes I've used
the
first currency.

I've imagined time
can pass.

I've made
men real
by touching
them
& briefly thought
it would
not
kill us all.

Eight Months Without

The sun on acid

a day so hot it buries its young

before they blink &

me over here forgetting.

Forgetting so I can remember

& keep forgetting.

The first man that laid hands

on me was a perfect shadow. &

the second & seventh & the tenth. What

if I've had my fill? Is there

such a thing? The sun still

full of itself burnt so bright

I turn cold—I am not

asking for much, just to never

live like I was. When I close

my eyes I feel like a scraped knee,

broken skin forever at the moment

it collides with dirt, awestruck

& fresh.

Saint Loss

Fall walks in on broken legs.
Fall walks in on hunger. Leaves red
as the throat of the girl who knows
how to beg.

Says, *have you proved your worth today?*
Says, *do you remember last year,*
the lace crossed tights, cold blue, the desperate men
unrolling like a long storied tongue? I—

I swaddle hell like a baby. Is there
any other way? I hold it close, we coo—

Wound Song

You've got childbearing hips, my rapist said.

Are we back to this? Am I still remembering?

The body a vessel for exchange as well as crime.

The body a vessel for the past as well as crime.

When I open my eyes to a new man, I have no idea how to judge.

Still keys between my fingers, the bleached moon a memory.

Hey. Can you hear me? *You've got childbearing hips*, my rapist said.

It's the last thing I remember after saying *No*.

girl, as it had to be then

all of my dice scattered rolled lonely / once

you pushed up against me in a motel shower,

storm clouds unraveling into storm,

my despair a last supper I kept attending against

all odds / & if I'd known what to invoke,

I might've / & if I'd known which plate to clean,

I might've / later you & me both on a sort of

cosmic inventory, it was how I'd always done it, but

imagine how it feels to count / the years demanded

a ceasefire but I kept hissing *wind wind wind*

The Anatomy, Ripened

Each night a swallow of a previous

I have lain in the cardinal red

My hands pressure points—they remember
their failures

The doorknobs they failed to reach
The men they failed to push
The flesh they failed to tear away (their
own)

I never meant to be the bird opened
Its feathers in every local mouth

Shut the door he said

Then he said then
he said—they lined up
like greedy marionettes
All of us on this stage

Morning is such a questionable state
For some of us it never comes

Life Cycle of an Ideology

The girl, lying, light pricking her eyes like pine needles.
Scene one: Creating empathy. Scene one: Creating victimhood.
No. A falsity. A rock in the throat.

The girl, older, still singing the same song.
Is it rewarding? Is god in a language?
No. A falsity. A rock in the throat.

broken bones

set blue set red set into twilight—I travel alone

> I've asked to not travel but that doesn't work; I've asked to hang
>> a wreath at a door, any
>> door, but the wood collapses & the flowers trail into dust—

if you are listening, thing they call god,

if you are speechless, busy rubbing the earth soft-hearted
> & missing, & missing
> so many spots,

know my many questions for what they are.

Seven Months Without

I meant to look for a solid patch, I meant

    to inhabit moments without seeking a promise

they'll pass. But the holograms were getting

    hungry, the ones I always fit into, & who

was I to judge? Elsewhere, I picked up

    & left. I could almost hear my old self breathing,

smell her warm & spoiled path.

Twenty-Eight

Throwing rocks at the stars saying *self don't be lonely.*

All the small things weighed easily as rain.

Half-committed to this moment & my values.

Half-aligned with the landscape's stark.

Honey, step in, the water's fresh, is a way to feel.

Someone suggested walking towards revealing

rather than persuasion. Somewhere, amidst all

the other words & the other minds, I am here,

tepid & shifting, but here.

Leash

A long extinct smell in the body, of the body.
A girl with hands raised, not in rapture.
They say the boxes we build close around us, but how,
then, do ghosts & stray blades of sun get in? A girl
rumored extinct, evading the rituals that preserve her.
A girl with a long mind, asking that same nuanced question,
haunted by sensory memory (smashed bones, red wine,
the gaping eyes, stench of force): *do we survive?*

Coming of Age

A body under duress knows it's a body

A body in the middle of a pendulum has no idea

My pulse unspooled

Who has not laid above themselves

Who has not said nothing

As another body pushes into it, makes claims

Who has not regarded hunger as a rotten peach

Well, this is as close as I'll get the thought

White light pouring in

A pain, too

Prayer Blankness

In the space before surgery.

The head round, thick, asking for a stay

against itself. I have been blood

& bloodlet. I have followed my family

to the pasture of *no god* or *this god*,

the grass chewy as cud. The heart

chewy as cud. *Ascetic or sensualist,*

they say. Like we get to choose

ourselves. The knife nears, no doctor.

I have been sober eight years.

What am I still doing here, to myself?

This Infinite Gap

We do it anyway, that which burns in us.

We raise a glass to nothingness
we imagine connection.

What part of you needed this part of me?

When I lie awake, at night, is the tragedy
in the milkless hollows of my bones
or somewhere stranger, a flatlands
you live & live & don't know you live—

No, stranger, I can't be a home nobody's built.

We tip the glasses, we miss our throats.

Between Seasons

All I can think about is how rare love is.

I don't mean it sadly. I just mean it.

The earth outside is so gorgeous

but too hot to step into. Florida, August.

I am circling my heart like a dog

ready to trap its prey. I keep

hearing these beautiful bird calls

& the sunlight through the window,

beautiful, & the trees through

the sunlight through the window,

beautiful too, but I am here inside.

Getting Over

Love grows slowly or love says *fuck that*.
Sometimes I stay feeling radical.
Sometimes the story I want to tell
stresses relief instead of loss. The man
is not central. The man is not central.
The man is already fading, leaves
out of season, the cold cracking
them underfoot. I live in a city
with no winter, but there is still cold.
Sometimes I call this space the clearing,
the absence house, & I thank god
waiting is no passive verb.
Do you hear that? Every bird
that's ever flown south for warmth
is still flying, still flying,
their wings in my head.

In Absentia

The hard part is the thickening of bones, the rebuilding
what only existed ever in a system of impulse say   say you want a
    cigarette
ten years later   say the elements that bind you
to your old self hold the lighter   flick it on easy everything
everything it says *used to come easy*   once you were raw, & the
    hells
you hounded   which were the dogs & which were the scent
    it all comes back
you know so easy   *everything* it says *could come easy*   &
    once the morning
breaks   yellow hard over your skin   you know how to push
    it back
you know it says *exactly how to swim*   *so come back*   *come*
    back there's still ocean

Centrifugal Hardship

I've been writing this eulogy that's run

out of words, that's asking another voice

to respond, I've been bathing in salt water

& trying to drink my spit, I've been as stable,

you know, as someone like me can be,

but that's the eulogy: for me, for what

I thought was a part but I can't seem to shed.

All problems eventually end a man says.

He burns a cigarette, he finishes the sentence

for somebody else, someone who listens.

II.

Time Stop

PORTRAIT: MATERNAL INSTINCT

In a second, I'd let the wind eat you, her mama said, singing like a lullaby. *In a second, gone your flesh, your guts, whatever pulses in your brain.* No. She was the mama, humming. She held her baby like a bunch of dried petals to scatter: precious, miniscule, designed to scatter for a greater purpose. *Oh, honey,* she said. The night late enough & all she wanted, really, was coming. She was the mama, she reminded herself. She kissed her daughter goodnight & laid her in the crib. Her daughter stared at her, so strange, so intense already—she reminded her of a cat, wondered if her blue eyes would trickery into another shade as she grew. In her universe, there is no questioning her reaction. The repulsion was love, & the love borne of a desire never divorced from distrust.

Sometimes they blurred into each other, all the figures—her daughter, her father, the siblings she raised, her mother collapsing, her husband drunk, again, needing dinner. Her husband drunk, again, falling asleep into dinner. But she never minded, not that much. She couldn't say she minded anything. It was afternoon & she was having a glass of bourbon & wondering about all these birds outside. The whiskey burned & she considered how comfortable it was to not have a center. She was all of those people falling out of her one by one. *In a second, I'd feed you to the sparrows*, she sang, although her baby was not in her arms, not even in the room, & the sparrows weren't nearly as hungry as her.

She was singing again, always singing, but nobody heard her. In her sleep she sang, as she cleaned she sang, as she pushed down thoughts she sang sang sang. The skylight above her billowing as she smeared herself awake & then asleep. This was the dream, wasn't it? Did she want more than a shadow man with his large large mouth, children to rotate & arrange? When she was young, she used to open her eyes wider & wider when fear appeared. She'd imagine them popping out, cupping a spoon behind their gooey backs. As she was older now, she required more difficult tactics.

Head underwater, life like a show canceled years in advance. *Where are you taking me?* she asked herself over & louder, practicing her face of silenced but still aggressive despair. *In a second, in a second*, she'd start to sing. The years rolled by like nausea. She cries, once, to her daughter, cries that she drinks too much. Her daughter opens her mouth & she rights herself to her throne of rage. It's never been, though, that she was inhumane. Just underwater, just from a distance, just this unjust world & she forgot how to swim.

How do the hours do? She stands up, sits down, stands up. Her daughter is young, she's rocking her to sleep, moving in the solemn rhythm long after her baby is dreaming. The moon outside like a greedy star, needing more light, more attention, more more more than the rest. When she wakes up tomorrow, she promises herself, she won't feel a thing more than what she wants to. It's possible all she has ever known are lullabies. The cicadas have emerged from their holes: they're all out tonight, crying, & she takes some strange satisfaction in their calls. They have such plain *purpose*. She sleeps with their aches.

In the middle of darkness, jerked awake. Fear pounding, heart in gasp. For what? *Oh, stop it*, she chides herself. The ceiling fan cuts air like an incessant rebuke. The man next to her, he lies still, sometimes he snores. *It is enough*, she thinks, *to have something to protect*. She gets up & gets busy, instead of. She practices *instead of.* Her baby is older or younger. The sun finally roasts the night like a marshmallow & she has been up, she has been ready, fist in hand, hand in throat. The ordinary will not be an ambush, she is resolute. She will be on the offensive, always. Then, in the midst of theoretical rigidity, she develops a love for birds. Can name them. The tufted titmouse is her favorite: what a name. It chirps & her tender spot pulses. She is here to love. She just knows love as warfare. It is midmorning & she is tired, wary, & should tend to her baby.

Some go to church. She's been, she remembers the aisles, her mother's funeral. How she had to take charge, she believed, so young & so flimsily engaged in vulnerability. The siblings came to her or she taught them to. She's reminiscing, watching the curtains flutter gently in the dusk. Her baby has been grabbing lately, reaching for everything, trying to eat what she can touch. The mama untangles hair from chubby fingers, necklace, face. Sometimes she hates it when this warm flesh meets hers: she grows claustrophobic, possessive of herself. *In a second, I'd feed us all,* she sings, leaving the sentence unfinished in a moment of gentleness.

Honey? It's someone else's voice, but she is groggy. She is not cruel: she is groggy. They live out in the semi-woods, enough nature that all she first startles aware of is the frogs. Bullfrogs, she thinks, with those lumbering bodies, bulging green growths, like disfigured dirt & moss. She admires them. *Honey?* The voice probably has reason, due cause, a correct aim. It's just hard with this sludge in the head, this exhaustion, this thirst, these currents of bourbon & self-sufficiency sloshing. Where is her baby? She envies.

Don't be unsympathetic, she coaches her baby, *or you'll be lonely.* Sometimes she stands in front of the refrigerator at night & holds her baby's bottles, imagining a softer life for herself. Imagining for herself. Sloshing: it's such a great, true verb. She keeps the whiskey under the sink, it keeps her inside herself. A cardinal perches on the magnolia tree hovering above the kitchen window. She is washing dishes now, unaware if they were already clean. Sometimes she keeps the radio on so she can hear ideas. In a few years she will tell her baby she is practical, not a feelings person.

Has the phone been ringing? Is that what woke her? She is in a permanent state of just waking, except when she is so awake it hurts, exhausts her bones, fixes her in perpetual sharpness. These are rules & they get confusing so they must be accepted & quickly forgotten. *Sweet little pumpkin pie,* she calls her baby today, surprising herself. Only she is allowed to surprise herself. She exhales as much as she inhales, or tries to. She never asked for redemption, but likely she deserves some. Her baby's eyes sometimes look like those snow globes they sell in department stores, easily shaken, everything settling below. *Sweet little sweet little sweet little pumpkin pie.*

There is a body, too, that holds her. Sometimes she claims it. Other times, well, other times. It's not that she doesn't believe in god. She does believe in errands. *All I know how to do is feed*, she sings, *I am the mama, I am the mama*. Her daughter gurgles up laughter, oddly. Although it's pre-language days & any response is odd, she finds this comforting. Not to be the superstitious type, to attach meaning to unmeaningful events: oh no, she must stay logical. A fox has been creeping through the yard lately, she's afraid it'll go after the cats. But really, what can she do? *If I see it, I'll shoot it*, she tells her husband. He has worked very many hours of manual labor & is so tired, he falls asleep into his plate of spaghetti. They both drink but not together, usually.

What about daytime? What about it? When else can she flurry. If someone is performing work, she is, too. Until the sweet gasp of whiskey, until she hollows the tree of her conception of self & drinks its sap. Then she works at her true work. She's been letting her baby sleep through the night more, but she still rushes awake imagining cries. Sometimes it's a barn owl, sometimes just the fact of her own existence, her rent on this planet. Must everything carry a weight? *Sleep now, little mama*, she sings to herself, *mama bear, mama bear*.

If her baby wanted the proper things, she would kill to provide. This is one emblem, one aspect of her loyalty. Once, when mad, she reminded herself of a fire hydrant. She's seen films where a burst hydrant brings joy, children dancing, playing in the street. No representation of reality is reality, though, she can tell you that. Suffering is also a prerequisite for punishment, she will say. She will be the good one, she decided once. She will care for the others. She will live in a country of no questions asked.

Her boredom god's boredom. We are almost done. A rubik's cube halved & halved & halved: she is her own puzzle, if only she could agree to play. The bourbon comes earlier, the baby comes with more weight, frustration. How little it resembles a trophy. When she was younger, she could daydream. It was the strangest gift, one she didn't realize she'd lost until it was years gone.

She belongs to her own government, the government of liquor & half-set suns. That's the time when things fall into place: she moves from one series of motions into the slowing one, like a blanket of sand sinking grain by grain over her body. She tells herself her baby won't hate her, later, for this. She tells herself she won't hate herself, later, for this. But of course much of her already does. *Wake up, little baby, the sky is falling*, she whispers, *& I'll find a way to make it your fault.*

He's brushing a hair off her face, in her dream. He's employing tenderness. She's struggling to remember who he is. Her husband, she thinks, in the way someone might look at a chessboard & see one of the front line, the pawns. So basic in design, so few nuances. Or maybe a knight—important but not overly so. She can't play chess, anyway, detests finishing games. Still, the touch—she remembers it when she wakes, it haunts her for a while after. So much of her waking is filled with ghost hours, ghost moments. *Who are you*, she sings to her baby, *who are you & what have we done?*

III.

Summers, Springs

Goodbye

The light a broken sonata, unfinished, too full of air,
too likely to illuminate—

I'm dreaming again. Just now
I tumbled awake from another love story
full of anger. Do I want too much, in my wanting
to want less?

Some things seem so simple. I turn on the tap
& water flows. Life fidgets everywhere. But me,

but me.

Impossibilities roost. Impossibilities caw.
The light, still unyielding, presents no new angles.
That's your job it says, widening,
loosening.

The particular fragile weight of redirection

is no exact science. For years I felt nothing in the wrong moments
except heavy a heavy ball not even wrecking.

At 27 I learned a man could ask before he touched me.

At 15 I learned a body could slice itself indefinitely,
could tear away a limb &   follow it: o reader,
            o reader, hell is the ricochet effect—

it took a long time & it still takes.

No volta, no simplicity. A series of thin nouns, rubbed raw. I guess
the best way to explain it (other
than not at all) is

how this morning, before a hurricane hit town, the birds
& what they carried in their beaks.

Short Sleeve Weather

So I broke a thicket in the house   So I laid fresh

across it like a prophet   Once, no metaphor, I

came in from the woods with my legs remade red

I was young, I hadn't felt a thing   Once my father

cut the ends off his fingers &, having forgotten

to take the fingertips to the hospital, left them in the yard

for the foxes, but I thought the deer would get there

first   They said I mistook everything

for a carnivore   O but I knew how to open

a bottle cap how to bloody my knuckles how to spin

through creek wilds   O I did it even when I sat, later,

whiskeybrained & deadthin listening to daytime owls

& letting X mark the stop that marked the spot that marked

the summer I lost my body under a *no* & a man's dark heft

Requiem Requiem

A girl once turned away from a fire &
later, fire turned from the girl—

have you ever lost the needle to your soul?
Easy question hard answer,

o, but it's not love I forsake, the girl says,
we weren't supposed to get confused about that.

Dear Better Self

They say love is a series of requests towards change,
or maybe I do. They say start by coughing out the grit

from your own lungs, but maybe that's me, too. Of course
I am the cat & its neck-severed bird, but god forbid

I become the mouth, again, too. Let the mouth operate
independently. Let me no more know the wanting

of a head released towards the quiet, quiet stars.

Continuance

Hope like a rodent walking through my head.

So long they said *when you're older.* I'm older

& I know as much as I know & still I get out of bed.

The sun knitting bright, its needles caught

on a Florida porch. *I have a feeling* I say.

& that's how every story starts: a piercing,

a breathing, an unfixed believing.

Poem, Tentative

Outside of my comfort zone, a wide eagle in the half-moon's fluorescence.

A longstanding breath. The arrogance of me & me & me

every time I *really think I know.* But maybe, in this galaxy,

I'll be given this chance. Not to disappear & not to capture.

To say to the birds, to all the birds, *I'm okay right here,*

since facing the gulf is far divorced from numbness at the gulf.

Twelve Months Without

I have this image you will make things better & then I meet you.

I wear, strangely, hope for a face. It rains, it accumulates distance

from a home system. Where is the map, the sun-twinged eyes?

All week I breathe myself in like a charm. Today I wake

sleeping back to back with the cat. We are concerned about intimacy,

we are holed up in these tendrils of solemnity & half-instinct.

Make a sudden noise. See which animals in us come out.

Pace

I wake up how a thief wakes up, one want at a time.

But I'm no longer insane. But the biggest electricity

holds a slow burn. If I had a daughter,

I'd hold her, I'd listen to her breathing & tell her

Honey

I'd tell her

Honey

there's no road long enough

to outlast your legs, & maybe she'd open those daughter eyes

so I wouldn't have to finish the sentence,

tell her of all the hurts & holes she'll have to scramble

around & finally just lie in, sometimes, the sun

as it is, giving it time, so up ahead the road has a chance

to stop looking the same.

Servant to Uncertainty

Let them eat desire & eat & eat—
what came first, the emotion
or the flawed system? I know
how to put a man up my nose,
how to only crave the end of me.
God, you gave me a world in decay
& so I demanded legs. *Let them eat
need* & eat & eat—god, you are
so weird. You made this ocean
that pulls & pulls & then pushes.

If Cut, You Bleed Moonlight

Later, coming from a position of not talking.

The air fresh, honest & open.

Everything like a window into a fall night.

One candle burning beside a lower one.

Thank god, right? Thank god.

You have never so deeply needed space.

You wrestled space, you pinned space

under the abs of men, you let men

take up eat up fuck up space—then, later,

like a wild animal given a lullaby.

A great temporary thing, like us all.

Mingling with the Possible Enemy

If we can disagree I appreciate.

If we can let our hands build a new, a safe fire.

I'm getting tired. My head is drifting into itself.

The interesting thing about having an experience

is that nobody can invalidate it.

Argument in a Wind Tunnel

I could, laying a hatchet in my head, say *it's all the same.*

I could, hatching the split, say *everything ebbs & flows,*

so do nothing. But even the wild pulses of cars

driving by the Florida highways know better.

Our eyes are what we've got for flora

& fauna some days, grandma, grandpa,

ancestors of thick-lidded, sedentary planting.

The gardens *are* loosening. *Movement*

isn't always circuitous, I argue, & a guillotine

of light cuts through the blinds & lands on my wrists.

The Road Ahead

My mother gave me my vocabulary
& my thirsts & my blames Say
grifter Say *radical* Say anything
in sotto voce

Any organ turns brown
submerged long enough in a whiskey glass
It's a law It's a family Say *do what I do*
because I will say
nothing

I have spoken & small continents have shifted

Other times, my words as thick
as the skulls they swim in Say *no,*

god is not a pitcher plant
It's us humans that eat each other

We Need a New Medium

We need new heads, angles at which to turn them & turn them & turn.

A husband, somewhere, on a wave, claiming he carries the ocean.

Our nails now scratch not poems but blood into gray walls.

We have tried you, language, but you have not been enough.

A boyfriend, somewhere, proving a closed heart gets fed.

All the wives' tales are backwards. All their homes are aflame.

What harbor do I stay away from? His, his, theirs—

Accident Report

Our heads, sweet-ish, sought pillows.

Light bent itself to get through the barred windows,
even in night, even alone,

a single prophecy of light wondering
if it was insane, to keep going.

The world outside set itself
like the broken bone it was,

but it had no doctors, & it did
what we all do with no expertise

& scrappy, childish pride—
it made new hurts, defended the wounds.

We Are Almost All the Same

but when I lick my lips, it's to soothe, not to catch drops of blood.

I reach for X to expel the catacombs in my head. I say *make whole*

these bones & society's grazing. X & its full-bellied eyes watch me

watch. It says *you know what's out there, it'll always be out there.* Still

I hand X a song I wrapped around a carcass. At least there's music,

can I catch a break with that? *No X exists to lighten your load*, X

caws, its voice catching on the lives in its throat. What a drink

the external always is, fast & sugary & —fast.

Owning

If you don't believe in blood loss you shouldn't carry blood.

I asked a man to carry me the moon & he said *undeserving*.

you or me? I asked, but the point was moot, of course

it was us both, it was a relationship built

on inhuman requests. *trauma* is *an object that rearranges*, I said.

softly then loudly, like a stone skipping towards.

I'll concede we all begin with the same wound. but from there

we are altered.

Self Portrait in a Swamp

I have lost everyone I needed to lose or keep,

at different hours—I have bound myself

like a spider to the plants that sought

to chew my bones to hollow— & yet,

a searchlight shredding & shining,

my internal landscape full-blooded &

new-blooded, & yet— any song

is a fight against silence, or so

I'd like to be told, there is so much

I'd like to be told, I have almost enough courage

to keep walking myself home

Some Yearning

I read a book where a man sees fruit ripening everywhere & forgives

his missing parents but my tendrils are so different, much starker—

I often forget, even, to eat. I give myself away on coffee & the thin promise

of usefulness, wishing I could be mist above a newborn sunrise,

helping it split open gently—forgive me, earth, I keep trying to be

not quite of you. There's a fullness to my heart when I stop

calculating its emptiness, I know, but I so often hold myself to some kind

of standard—call it an unkindness of the self, call it the skeletons of a larger

creature I keep forgetting I am not, call after it, like a cat might *mrrr* softly

at the food bowl where his littermate used to eat, newly absent after a decade

of unfathomable companionship—call after me, call after me like that.

Acknowledgments

Thank you to everyone who has helped my poems & I along the way. It would be impossible to list all of those people—it's probable I don't even know all of them, as this life gifts me with more than I can recognize or comprehend. Here are just a few of the most important voices, poetically & otherwise, that I'm privileged to hear: Anna Rose Carson, Jen Charles, Chantal Fortin, Sharon Hartman, Jon (Jawn) Knapp, Jane Lee, Adriane Liedy, Zach Linge, Margaret Mauk, Nate & Gohan McConnell, David McNeil, Merrell McQueen, Tara Mae Mulroy, Dyan Neary, Bill Sharpe, Diana Stoen, Ashley Weaver, & Paul Zammit.

Thank you to my PhD committee: Jimmy Kimbrell, Andrew Epstein, Juan Carlos Galeano, Barbara Hamby, and Diane Roberts. Thank you also to some of the best of FSU: Kaveh Akbar, Kelly Butler, Marianne Chan, Bella Chan-McGilligan, Alexa Doran, Minnie Fargason-Marotta, Tiffany Isaacs, Chris Jensen, Paige Lewis, Colleen Mayo, Jayme Ringleb, & Kelsey Ward.

Thank you, of course, to Diane Goettel, Kit Frick, & everyone at Black Lawrence Press.

Thank you to my parents and grandmother, my cats Joy G. Baumann & Louise C. Baumann, my ex-foster kittens, my yard possum & Cutie Pie the outdoor cat.

Photo: Kenneth L. Johnson

Ruth Baumann is the author of *Parse* (Black Lawrence Press, 2018). She is also the author of five chapbooks, including *A Thousand Ars Poeticas* (Sixth Finch, 2018), *Retribution Binary* (Black Lawrence Press, 2017), & *I'll Love You Forever & Other Temporary Valentines* (Salt Hill, 2015). She holds a PhD from Florida State University and an MFA from the University of Memphis. Poems are published in *New South, Prairie Schooner, Third Coast* & more listed at www.ruthbaumann.com.